Donut Dilemma

written by
Mary E. Ryan

illustrated by
Colleen Muske

www.keeneditions.com

"It's an exciting day, kindergartners," said Mrs. Knickerbocker. "We're celebrating 'Donuts with Dads' next week and it's time to make our invitations."

Nan and her best friend, Sophie, got busy with their papers and markers. Sophie nudged Nan and whispered, "You can't come, Nan, you don't have a dad."

Sawyer, who loved to bug the girls, shouted, "Hey Nan, you *have* to have a dad. *Everyone* has to have a mom *and* a dad."

"My dad can't come," said Charlie. "He lives too far away."

"Yah, but you still *have* a dad," said Sawyer.

Seeing the hurt look on Nan's face, Mrs. Knickerbocker clapped her hands and said, "Kindergartners, pay attention to your own work."

Nan scribbled on her paper and tried *really* hard not to show anyone how mad she was. She didn't want to work on this dumb invitation anymore. She just wanted to be home with Mom.

When the school bell rang at the end of the day, Nan ran out the front door to where her nanny, Reecie, was waiting. Nan burst into tears. "Soph says I can't go to 'Donuts with Dads' because I don't have a dad. It's not fair!" she cried.

Reecie pulled Nan into her arms and said, "Okay, bud, let's go home and talk to Mom. I'm sure she'll know what to do."

With that, Reecie and Nan headed for home.

Nan *knew* she didn't have a dad. "You and I are a team, Nan," Mom always told her. But now Nan was confused. It seemed like their team was missing someone.

Mom was at work in her office when Reecie dropped Nan off after school. "Hi, Sweet Pea, come and give your mom a big squeeze. It's the *best* part of my day!"

Every morning when Nan left for school, Mom gave her a kiss and said, "Let's make it the best day ever."

And for Nan, almost every day *was* the best day ever. But not today. Not even the big, sloppy kiss from her dog, McKinley, made Nan smile.

"I know I don't have a dad, Mom, but Soph said I can't come to 'Donuts with Dad' at school, and then Sawyer said in front of the *whole* class, '*Everyone* has to have a mom *and* a dad.' What about *me*, Mom, why don't I have a dad?"

"Oh, sweetie," said Mom. "Let's get you a snack and have a little chat."

With that, Mom, Nan and, of course, McKinley started to sort things out.

"Sawyer is a little bit right and a little bit wrong," Mom said. "You don't have a dad like Sophie and Sawyer, but it *does* take both a man and a woman to make a baby.

"With us, Doctor Deb and a man we've never met helped me have you, but that doesn't make that man your dad. It takes lots of love to make someone a mom or a dad."

Nan's face got all scrunchy because she was thinking *very* hard. "Is that why we pray for the good man and Doctor Deb every night before bed?"

"That's right," said Mom. "When I was a little girl I dreamed of falling in love and being a mom just like my mom, your Grammy Nancy. But things didn't happen that way, and I couldn't wait one more second to find my way to you.

"So the *best* part of my dream came true. I got you! I love you with my whole heart, and I know for sure you and I are meant to be a family."

"Hey, what about Reecie?" asked Nan. "Is *she* part of our family? Cuz I love Reecie, too."

"Of course, she is," said Mom. "The cool thing is how many people love us. Lots of cousins, awesome aunts and uncles, the best neighbors in the world...and we have Reecie! So we have a *really* big circle of love."

"Don't forget Grammy Nancy," said Nan. "I'm the Nan part of Nancy."

"That's right," said Mom. "Grammy died before you were born, but she would have loved you to pieces, too."

"I hope not," giggled Nan, "cuz I like being whole."

Just then, the phone rang and Mom answered it. She listened for a minute. "Sounds good," she said, nodding her head. She handed the phone to Nan. "It's Mrs. Knickerbocker. She has something to tell you."

Now it was Nan's turn to listen. Pretty soon Mom saw Nan start to smile. A BIG WIDE no-front-tooth smile.

Nan hung up the phone and twirled around.

"Mrs. Knickerbocker has a great idea, Mom. Instead of having donuts just with dads, we're having a 'Donut Day,' and we can invite anyone we want!"

Nan ran to her backpack and pulled out the wrinkled invitation. She held it up and said, "We're making new invitations tomorrow, and *I'm* going to have donuts with Uncle Dave!"

Nan knew that even though she didn't have a dad, her Uncle Dave would *love* to come with her. She giggled, because she had *lots* of uncles to choose from, but it was her Uncle Dave who *really* loved donuts!

"You know what, Mom, you're right. We *are* a team, a *great* team!"

Dedicated to:

the "real" Nan —
You have no idea how much joy you give your mom and the rest of us in your very large circle of love.

my sister, Jean —
Thank you for having the courage to chart a new course for yourself by bringing Nan into this world. Mom and Dad would be so pleased.

and Ann —
This story is only a book because of you. You guided my voice and gave me courage. I am humbled by your talent and forever grateful for your friendship.